THE STORY OF KWANZAA

by Donna L. Washington
illustrated by Stephen Taylor

HarperCollins*Publishers*

This book is dedicated to my mother—
she taught me how to make dreams live
—D.L.W.

To my family and friends and all the souls
who made this whole process materialize
—S.T.

The illustrations in this book were done with acrylic, pastels,
and gouache on illustration board. The borders were created
by photographing contemporary African fabrics.

The Story of Kwanzaa
Text copyright © 1996 by Donna L. Washington
Illustrations copyright © 1996 by Stephen Taylor
Printed in the U.S.A. All rights reserved.

Library of Congress Cataloging-in-Publication Data
Washington, Donna, date
  The story of Kwanzaa / by Donna L. Washington ; illustrated by Stephen Taylor.
    p.   cm.
  Summary: Describes the traditions and customs of Kwanzaa and includes activities.
  ISBN 0-06-024818-1. — ISBN 0-06-024819-X (lib. bdg.)
  1. Kwanzaa—Juvenile literature.   [1. Kwanzaa.]   I. Taylor, Stephen, date, ill.   II. Title.
GT4403.W37 1996   95-22356
394.2'61—dc20   CIP
                                                                              AC

Typography by Elynn Cohen and David Neuhaus
1   2   3   4   5   6   7   8   9   10
❖
First Edition

THE STORY OF KWANZAA

KWANZAA TIME has come at last. Now it is time to light the candles on the *kinara*. It is time to fly the *bendera*, listen to old stories from Africa, wear African clothes, and eat good food. It is time to make gifts for friends and celebrate the good things in all people.

Kwanzaa is not a religious holiday like Hanukkah or Christmas. Kwanzaa is an American festival that honors African America. It starts on December 26, the day after Christmas. It is a time when we stop and remember the past as we work together for the future.

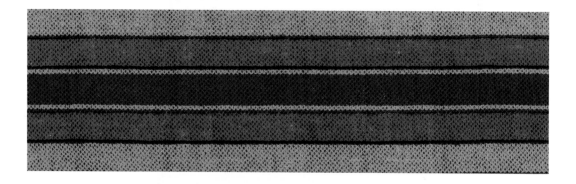

THE HISTORY

Some of our ancestors came from Africa. They were proud and beautiful people. Some of them lived in great kingdoms. Their rulers wore ivory, gold, and precious stones. They were great warriors. Some of them lived in smaller family groups. They traveled together with their livestock. Some lived in small villages or in the rain forests. They worshipped their own gods and had their own festivals and holy days. They made music and art and told the stories of their ancestors. When the Europeans came to Africa, all of that changed.

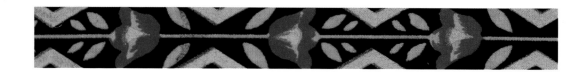

Many of the Africans were captured and taken away on ships. They did not know where they were being taken or what was going to happen to them. When they reached land, they were sold as slaves. Much of their traditions and history were lost.

The enslaved Africans created new traditions, and they made up new stories. Many of their stories were about a very smart rabbit. Bruh (shortened from "brother") or Brer Rabbit was very small, and always in trouble. Brer Rabbit did not use his muscle to escape his enemies—he used his brain. These stories were really about the slaves and the slave owners.

The enslaved Africans fought against slavery in many ways. In their stories they spoke of freedom. In their churches they sang beautiful spirituals about freedom. They even stole away north to freedom.

As time passed, many Americans began to see that slavery was wrong. America divided into two parts. In the Northern part of the country, many people were against slavery. In the Southern part, many people favored it. In the North, the people worked in factories and used machines. They did not need slave labor. In the South, the enslaved Africans worked on huge farms called plantations. The Southern farmers worried that if slavery ended, there would be no one to work in their fields. The North and South grew less and less friendly with each other.

When Abraham Lincoln became president, the Southern states feared he would tell them to free the slaves. They decided to secede from, or leave, the Union. They wanted to be their own country. America had a civil war. At the end of the war, the North and South reunited. Slavery was outlawed. The Africans were finally free.

The African Americans were free, but they did not have many of the civil rights offered to other Americans. Civil rights are the basic freedoms that every citizen in our country has. These rights were won for African Americans through the civil rights movement. Because of the work of many people, African Americans have the right to vote, attend any school or college, get good jobs, live where they want, and sit anywhere they choose.

Each new right was won only after great struggles. In 1966 a man named Dr. Maulana Karenga was one of the people involved in the civil rights movement. As part of his fight for African America he created a festival. He called this festival Kwanzaa.

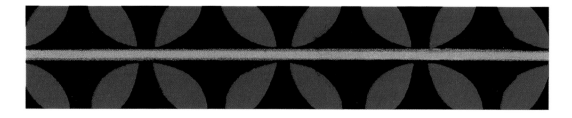

THE SEVEN DAYS OF KWANZAA

Kwanzaa is a word that comes from Swahili. It means "first fruits." It is a celebration of the bounty of the earth. Swahili is a language that is spoken all over eastern and central Africa. Dr. Karenga chose this language because he wanted African Americans to remember that the whole of Africa was their ancestral land, not just one country in Africa. Kwanzaa is based on many other first-fruit celebrations in Africa, but Dr. Karenga created this one for Africans in America.

Kwanzaa is based upon seven principles or beliefs. We call these beliefs the *Nguzo Saba*. There is one principle for each day of Kwanzaa. Even though we celebrate Kwanzaa only once a year, we are supposed to keep the principles of the *Nguzo Saba* every day of our lives.

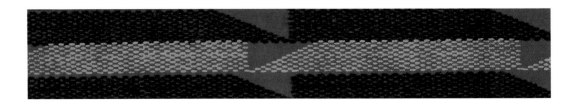

The first day of Kwanzaa is called *umoja*. That means unity. Only by having strong families and creating a community will African Americans be able to maintain unity.

The second day is *kujichagulia*. That means self-determination. People must stand up for themselves. They must tell others what they want. They must not let anyone else decide their future.

Ujima is the third day. We must work together and help each other. We must take responsibility for our problems and the problems of those around us, and help each other solve those problems.

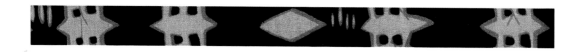

The fourth day is *ujamaa*. This means that we support African-American businesses.

The fifth day is *nia*. *Nia* means purpose. African Americans must make it their purpose to maintain the dignity of their ancestors. It is important to maintain families, build communities, attend colleges, and open businesses. Their purpose must be to claim their rightful place in the world.

Day six is *kuumba*. This word means creativity. Our ancestors made music, danced, and created beautiful works of art. It is up to us to create our own art. We must work to make our community proud. In the evening of *kuumba*, we celebrate the *karamu*. *Karamu* is the great feast of Kwanzaa.

The last day of Kwanzaa is *imani*. On this day we celebrate ourselves. Imani means faith. We must have faith in our own beliefs and in our abilities. We must have faith in each other and our dreams for the future.

GETTING READY FOR KWANZAA

THE TABLE ◆ There are some special things that belong on the table at Kwanzaa time. One of those things is a straw mat we call a *mkeka*. The *mkeka* reminds us of our traditions. It is a place to start building our future. The *mazao* and *muhindi* belong on top of the *mkeka. Mazao* are fruits and vegetables. They stand for unity. They represent the rewards of working together. *Muhindi* are ears of corn. There should be one ear of corn for each child in the family. Children are the center of the Kwanzaa celebration. They represent our hopes for the future.

THE CUP ◆ At Kwanzaa time, we share a unity cup. We call this cup the *kikombe cha umoja.* Everyone takes a sip out of it. It stands for our togetherness, or unity, the first principle of *Nguzo Saba*.

THE KINARA ◆ We also use a *kinara*, a candleholder, at Kwanzaa time. We call the seven candles *mishumaa saba*. They are red, green, and black. These are also the colors of the *bendera*. The *bendera* is the African-American flag. It was originally created by Marcus Garvey, a revolutionary who worked for the welfare of the African Americans. The red is for the blood of the African people, the black is for the face of the African people, and the green is the hope for new life. There is a proper way to set up the *kinara*. As you face the *kinara*, three red candles should be on your right, three green candles on the left, and a black candle in the middle. We light a candle for each day of Kwanzaa. On the first day we light the black one. On the second day we light the black one and a red one. On the third day we light the black one, a red one, and a green one. We continue this pattern until *imani*, when all the candles are lit. The *kinara* stands for the first African men and women.

THE CELEBRATION

There are many different ways to celebrate Kwanzaa. Many people start by asking, *"Habari gani?"* That means "What's the news?" Then someone, usually a child, answers with the *Nguzo Saba* of the day. Then you light the candles.

After you light the candles, you talk about the belief of the day. You might tell a folktale, talk about a famous African American, or tell how the *Nguzo Saba* affects your life. It should be a time to share your thoughts. You can stay home with your family, or find out what is going on in your community and join other people. After the candles and the sharing, people call *Harambee!* It means "Let's pull together!"

Food is a very big part of the celebration. Every night of Kwanzaa, you can try dishes from places where the ancestors of African Americans lived. One night you could have Zambian food. The next night you could have food from the Sudan. Then you could try Ghanaian food. This is a good way to warm up for the big night. *Karamu* should be a great feast.

On the night of *karamu*, there are many ways to enjoy the feast. You could have a dinner party or go to an African restaurant. This is a night you share with many people.

KARAMU

Karamu is a very special night. This is the night of the biggest party of Kwanzaa. One of the most important parts of *karamu* is the food. There should be a lot of food!

At the feast, there can be African and African-American music, dances, art, and stories. You could also have speeches. It is a celebration of African-American heritage. It is a time for people to tell others about themselves. It is a time to remember the people who have worked to make our lives better. It is a feast of the past and the present and our dreams for the future.

Kwanzaa is a celebration that asks all of us to take care of each other and honor ourselves. It is a time for friends, family, food, and fun! So light the candles! Fly the *bendera*! Eat!

KWANZAA YENU IWE NA HERI!
MAY YOUR KWANZAA BE A HAPPY ONE!

THINGS TO MAKE AT KWANZAA TIME

People exchange *zawadi* at Kwanzaa time. *Zawadi* are small gifts. They should be things that teach us about our African and African-American heritage. Many *zawadi* are homemade. They can be as simple as a poster with the *Nguzo Saba* written on it or little *bendera*s. Some people like to give fancier gifts, like African outfits or books. You can give one *zawadi* every day of Kwanzaa. Some people give gifts at Kwanzaa *karamu* instead of Christmas. The choice is yours.

COW TAIL SWITCH

In Africa, the people use something called a cow tail switch. It is made from a cow's tail and is used by important people, such as kings, queens, healers, and storytellers. It is a symbol of honor and respect. This is a *zawadi* you can make for someone important to you.

You will need:

a paper roll from paper towels
markers or paint
brown fabric or leather 3 inches
  wide
scissors
rubber cement
bright-colored leather or yarn

*beads
*bells
*shells (or glitter or pretty rocks)
 string
 thick wool (brown, white, or black,
   and the bulkier the better)

*Optional

1. Decorate the paper-towel roll with paint or markers in any design you like.

2. Cut the brown fabric or leather into a rectangle that will wrap around the top end of the towel roll once. Make sure that at least 2 inches of brown fabric sticks up over the top of the paper roll.

3. After you have cut the brown fabric, put some rubber cement on the bottom portion of the fabric. Then wrap the fabric or leather around the end of the towel roll, leaving the end open.

4. Cut the bright leather or yarn into 3 strings about 14 inches long.

5. Take out the beads, bells, and/or shells and the string. Cut a piece of string that is 14 inches long and string the beads, bells, and shells onto it. You want the beads to move and the bells to ring, so don't crowd your string.

6. This string is going to be part of the handle. Take the bright pieces of yarn and braid or twist them together with the string of beads and bells. When you have done this, tie off both ends.

7. Fold the handle over and glue it into the fabric or leather at the end of the switch. Glue the fabric closed.

8. Take the wool and cut it into strings about 28 or 30 inches long. Fold the wool in half and glue it into the bottom of the paper-towel roll.

9. Decorate the brown fabric or leather with shells. Now you have a cow tail switch!

Below is a recipe to get you started on your own Kwanzaa *karamu*.

BENNE CAKES

Benne cakes are a food from West Africa. *Benne* means sesame seeds. The sesame seeds are eaten for good luck. This treat is still eaten in some parts of the American South.

You will need:

oil to grease cookie sheet
1 cup of packed brown sugar
¼ cup of butter or margarine,
   softened
1 egg, beaten
½ teaspoon of vanilla extract

1 teaspoon of freshly squeezed lemon
   juice
½ cup of all-purpose flour
½ teaspoon of baking powder
¼ teaspoon of salt
1 cup of toasted sesame seeds

Preheat the oven to 325°. Lightly oil a cookie sheet. Mix together the brown sugar and butter, and beat until they are creamy. Stir in the egg, vanilla extract, and lemon juice. Add flour, baking powder, salt, and sesame seeds. Drop by rounded teaspoons onto the cookie sheet 2 inches apart. Bake for 15 minutes or until the edges are browned. Enjoy!

WORDS TO KNOW

bendera (behn-DEH-rah) ◆ The African-American flag

Habari gani? (hah-BAH-ree GAh-nee) ◆ "What's the news?"

Harambee! (hah-rahm-BEH) ◆ "Let's pull together!"

imani (ee-MAH-nee) ◆ faith (Day 7)

karamu (kah-Rah-moo) ◆ the feast

kikombe cha umoja (kee-KOM-beh-chah oo-MOH-jah) ◆ the unity cup

kinara (kee-NAH-rah) ◆ the candleholder

kujichagulia (koo-ji-chah-goo-LEE-ah) ◆ self-determination (Day 2)

kuumba (koo-OOM-bah) ◆ creativity (Day 6)

Kwanzaa (KWAHN-zah) ◆ first fruits

Kwanzaa yenu iwe na heri! (KWAhn-zah YEH-noo EE-weh nah HEH-ree) ◆
    "May your Kwanzaa be a happy one!"